G000020490

MATHWORDS

A word book for mathematics

Mathematics Project Officer: Carol Jenkins
Editorial Consultant: Dr Gareth Roberts
Illustrated by Anthony Evans

CAMBRIDGE
UNIVERSITY PRESS

Published by the Press Syndicate of the University of Cambridge
The Pitt Building, Trumpington Street, Cambridge CB2 1RP
40 West 20th Street, New York, NY 10011–4211, USA
10 Stamford Road, Oakleigh, Melbourne 3166, Australia

© Cambridge University Press 1994

First published 1994

Printed in Great Britain at the University Press, Cambridge

A Catalogue record for this book is available from the British Library

ISBN 0 521 45527 8

This book was developed by the Mathematics Project Officer at the
Language Studies Centre, Anglesey, with the assistance of Dr Gareth
Roberts, Mathematics Department, The Normal College, Bangor. This book
is part of the outcome of a project financed by the Welsh Office through the
Committee for the Development of Welsh Education.

Mathematics Project Officer: Carol Jenkins
Editorial Consultant: Gareth Roberts
Illustrations: Anthony Evans
Cover Illustration: Derk Matthews

Contents

Introduction

As a result of the many changes and developments that have occurred in the teaching and learning of mathematics during recent years, there have been more opportunities to discuss mathematics in the classroom. Time and time again, teachers' attentions have been drawn to the importance of encouraging children to discuss their work and to explain what they are doing. As the Cockcroft Report (*Mathematics Counts*, HMSO, 1982) states:

> Language plays an essential part in the formulation and expression of mathematical ideas. [para. 306]

> All children need, as a first stage in their learning of mathematics, to develop their understanding of words and expressions of this kind by means of activities and discussion in the classroom, and this development of mathematical language should continue throughout the primary years. [para. 307]

The National Curriculum for Mathematics also mentions the importance of language. Attainment Target 1 (Using and Applying Mathematics) notes that pupils should be able to:

* talk about their own work and respond to questions. [Level 1]

* talk about work or ask questions using appropriate mathematical language. [Level 2]

* use or interpret appropriate mathematical terms and mathematical aspects of everyday language in a precise way. [Level 3]

* examine and present findings using oral, written or visual forms. [Level 6]

The Non-Statutory Guidance for Teachers (Curriculum Council for Wales, 1989) states that:

> Through the medium of their mathematical studies, pupils should learn how to use mathematical language to describe and represent relationships, interpret events and make predictions. [Part A, page 3]

When discussing mathematics, it is important to be consistent in using the correct terms to ensure that children become familiar with them. The report *Mathematics from 5 to 16* (HMSO 1987) states that:

> In comparison with many other subjects there are relatively few technical terms in mathematics but difficulties often arise because much of this vocabulary is used so infrequently that it does not become an integral part of mathematical language and activity. In particular, pupils are done a disservice if specialised vocabulary is avoided, for example, if 'the top line of a fraction' is always used instead of 'numerator' and 'a four-sided figure' is constantly used instead of 'quadrilateral'. [para. 2.5]

It must also be remembered that there are several ways of expressing the same thing in mathematics. Paragraphs 307-310 of the Cockcroft Report deal with this variety of language and urge teachers to help children to became familiar with all forms of expression. But, as the pack written by the Gwynedd Education Authority PrIME Group (*Iaith a Mathemateg, Language and Mathematics*, Normal College, 1991) notes:

> Not all teachers accept this advice; they feel that sometimes, the use of a wide variety of language within mathematics tends to confuse young children. Nevertheless, one of the main aims of primary education is the development of children's language. One aspect of this task is to enable children to use A VARIETY OF MATHEMATICAL LANGUAGE WITH CONFIDENCE.

This book was designed, therefore, to help children develop their understanding of mathematical terms and expressions so that they may be able effectively to express and explain the work that they do. It is hoped that the book will be:

* of benefit to children at school and at home;

* of help to parents;

* useful to teachers in the classroom.

The vocabulary which appears in the book has been confined to the terms which are most likely to arise when mathematics is taught in the primary school (using Levels 1 to 6 of the National Curriculum as a rough guideline).

How to use *Mathwords*

The book has been divided into a number of sections. Within each section, there is one main drawing which depicts some mathematical terms together with a number of smaller drawings and definitions.

If you wish to discover the meaning of a word, you must, firstly, know to which section it belongs and on which page it appears.

* Look for the word in the index which starts on page 54. The index is in alphabetical order.

* Next to each word you will see the number of the relevant page (or pages).

* Turn to that page to find an explanation of that particular word.

The index will also tell you whether the word is a noun, verb, adverb, adjective or preposition.

Number

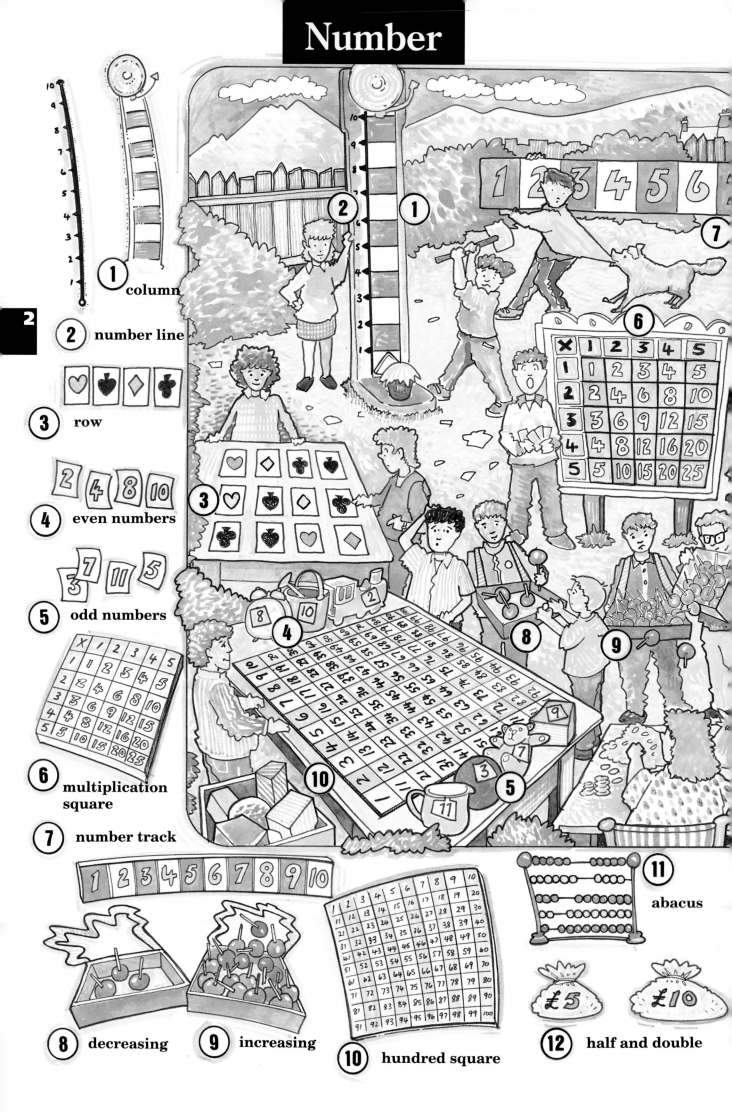

1 column

2 number line

3 row

4 even numbers

5 odd numbers

6 multiplication square

7 number track

8 decreasing

9 increasing

10 hundred square

11 abacus

12 half and double

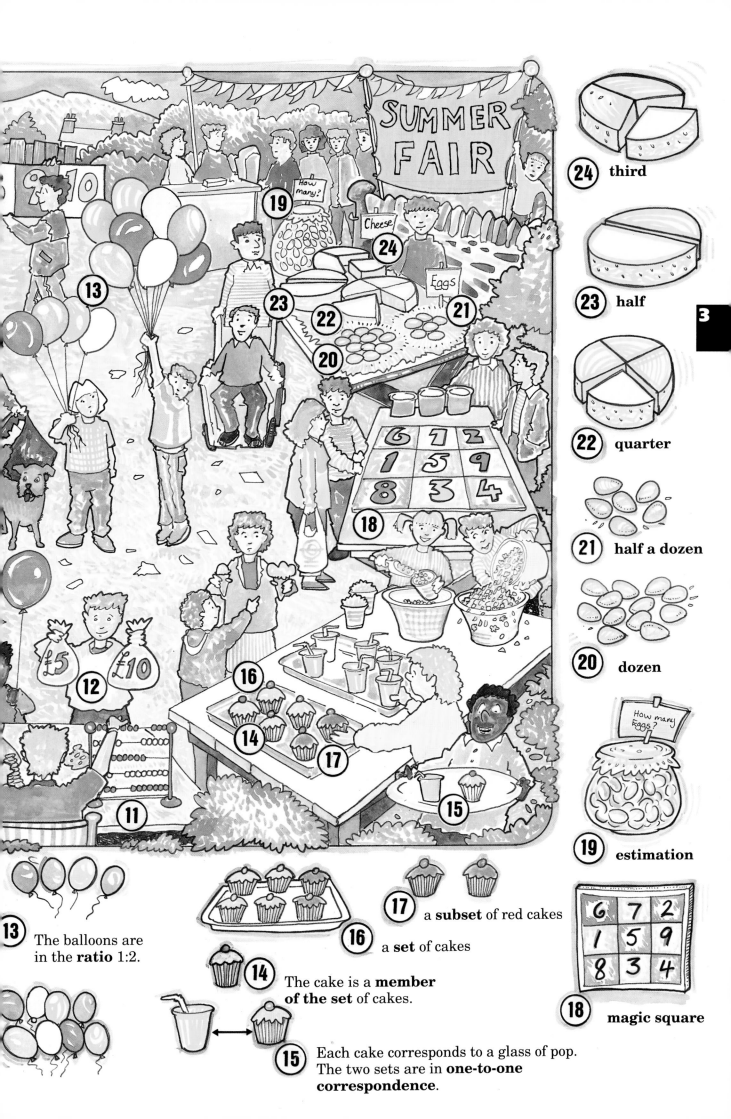

SUMMER FAIR

24 **third**

23 **half**

22 **quarter**

21 **half a dozen**

20 **dozen**

How many Eggs?

19 **estimation**

18 **magic square**

13 The balloons are in the **ratio** 1:2.

17 a **subset** of red cakes

16 a **set** of cakes

14 The cake is a **member of the set** of cakes.

15 Each cake corresponds to a glass of pop. The two sets are in **one-to-one correspondence**.

3

Cardinal Numbers

0	zero, nought, nil
1	one
2	two
3	three
4	four
5	five
6	six
7	seven
8	eight
9	nine
10	ten
11	eleven
12	twelve
13	thirteen
14	fourteen
15	fifteen
16	sixteen
17	seventeen
18	eighteen
19	nineteen
20	twenty
21	twenty-one
22	twenty-two
:	:
30	thirty
40	forty
50	fifty
60	sixty
70	seventy
80	eighty
90	ninety
100	one hundred
500	five hundred
1000	one thousand
1,000,000	million
1,000,000,000,000	billion

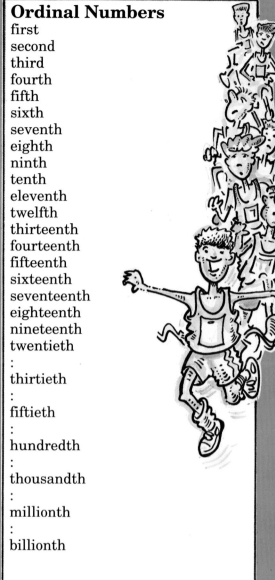

Ordinal Numbers

first
second
third
fourth
fifth
sixth
seventh
eighth
ninth
tenth
eleventh
twelfth
thirteenth
fourteenth
fifteenth
sixteenth
seventeenth
eighteenth
nineteenth
twentieth
:
thirtieth
:
fiftieth
:
hundredth
:
thousandth
:
millionth
:
billionth

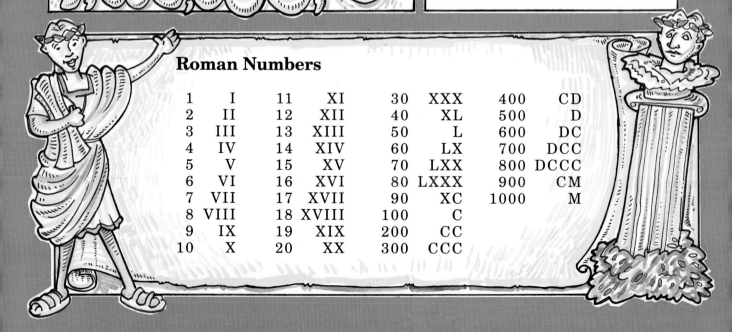

Roman Numbers

1	I	11	XI	30	XXX	400	CD
2	II	12	XII	40	XL	500	D
3	III	13	XIII	50	L	600	DC
4	IV	14	XIV	60	LX	700	DCC
5	V	15	XV	70	LXX	800	DCCC
6	VI	16	XVI	80	LXXX	900	CM
7	VII	17	XVII	90	XC	1000	M
8	VIII	18	XVIII	100	C		
9	IX	19	XIX	200	CC		
10	X	20	XX	300	CCC		

A **whole number** is a number which belongs to the set:

A **positive number** is a number greater than zero. For example,

A **negative number** is a number less than zero. For example,

An **integer** is a number which belongs to the set:

The **minus sign** (−) denotes that the number is negative.

A **plus sign** (+) can show that a number is positive.

Two divides exactly into every **even number**.

Two does not divide exactly into an **odd number**.

Consecutive numbers are numbers which follow each other in order. For example,

A **triangular number** is the number of dots in a triangular arrangement.

A **square number** is the number of dots in a square arrangement.
16 is a square number. We write $4 \times 4 = 4^2 = 16$.

The **square root** of 36 is 6 because $6 \times 6 = 36$. We write

8 is a **cube number** because $2 \times 2 \times 2 = 8$. We write

$$2^3 = 8$$

The **cube root** of 27 is 3 because $3 \times 3 \times 3 = 27$. We write

35 is a 2-digit number. 862 is a 3-digit number.

The ten **digits** of our number system are 0 1 2 3 4 5 6 7 8 9

5 is the **digital root** of 365 because when the digits are added we get

$3 + 6 + 5 = 14, 1 + 4 = 5$

A **palindromic number** is a number which reads the same from left to right and from right to left. For example,

353   16361

The numbers 1, 2, 4 and 8 divide exactly into 8.

The **factors** of 8 are 1, 2, 4 and 8

A **common factor** of two numbers is a number which divides exactly into them.

5 is a common factor of 15 and 40

A **prime number** is a number with only two factors, the number itself and 1.   For example,   2 13 29

A **multiple** of 5 is a number which is divisible by 5. That is any number in the 5 times table.

The multiples of 5 are 5, 10, 15, 20 ...

The **lowest common multiple (L.C.M.)** is the smallest number that any two numbers will divide into.

The L.C.M. of 6 and 5 is 30

The **sieve of Eratosthenes** can find all the prime numbers less than 100. On a 100 square, cross out the 1 and all the multiples of 2, 3, 5 and 7 (except for 2, 3, 5 and 7 themselves). The numbers which haven't been crossed out are the prime numbers.

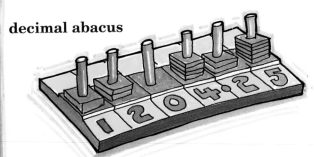

decimal abacus

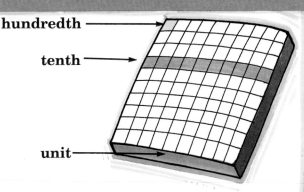

hundredth

tenth

unit

A **decimal number** is a number which contains
a whole part and a fractional part separated by a **decimal point**.
The position of each digit denotes its value.
378.21 is a decimal number.

Sometimes, the digits in a decimal number are repeated.
Such a number is called a **recurring decimal**.

$1 \div 3 = 0.3333333...$ We write $0.\dot{3}$
$3 \div 11 = 0.272727...$ We write $0.\dot{2}\dot{7}$

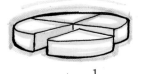

quarter $\frac{1}{4}$

half $\frac{1}{2}$

third $\frac{1}{3}$

Some everyday **fractions**.

A **fraction** is a **part** of something whole, or a number less than 1.

The **denominator** is the bottom number of a fraction which
tells us how many equal parts the shape has been divided into.
5 is the denominator in the fraction $\frac{3}{5}$.

The **numerator** is the top number of a fraction
which tells us how many parts are needed.
3 is the numerator in the fraction $\frac{3}{5}$.

Fractions are **equivalent** if they are the same size.
Equivalent fractions belong to the same
fraction family. For example, $\frac{1}{2} = \frac{2}{4} = \frac{4}{8}$.

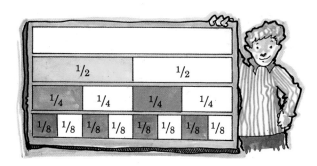

Before fractions may be added or subtracted, the
common denominator must be found. This is
the L.C.M. of the two denominators.
The common denominator of $\frac{2}{3}$ and $\frac{3}{4}$ is 12.

A **mixed number** is a whole number with
a fractional part. $2\frac{1}{4}$ is a mixed number.

In an **improper** (top-heavy) **fraction**, the numerator is greater
than the denominator. An improper fraction is greater than 1.
$\frac{7}{4}$ is an improper fraction.

A **percentage** is a fraction of
a hundred, such as $\frac{36}{100}$
(36 parts of a hundred or
36 hundredths).
We write 36%, or 36 **per cent**.

£5 is **half of** £10. £10 is **double** £5.

$4 \times 6 = 24$ is a multiplication. $28 - 13 = 15$ is a subtraction.
In a division, if the numbers do not divide exactly, the number left over is called the **remainder**: $17 \div 5 = 3$ remainder 2 (or 3 r 2)

This is the 3 **times table**:

$1 \times 3 = 3$ $3 \times 3 = 9$ $5 \times 3 = 15$ $7 \times 3 = 21$ $9 \times 3 = 27$
$2 \times 3 = 6$ $4 \times 3 = 12$ $6 \times 3 = 18$ $8 \times 3 = 24$ $10 \times 3 = 30$

8

In a **sequence** of numbers, the numbers all obey a specific rule.

DECREASE   ## INCREASE

2, 5, 8, 11, 14, ... In this sequence, the numbers **increase** in threes.

26, 21, 16, 11, ... In this sequence, the numbers **decrease** in fives.

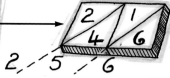

Napier's Bones are a set of rods used as an aid to multiplication. They were devised by John Napier, a Scottish theologian and mathematician.

Therefore,
$32 \times 8 = 256$

$7 + 3 = 10$
7 **add** 3 is 10
7 **plus** 3 is 10
the **sum** of 3 and 7 is 10
adding 3 to 7 gives 10
3 **more than** 7 is 10

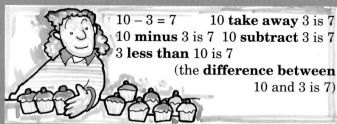

$10 - 3 = 7$ 10 **take away** 3 is 7
10 **minus** 3 is 7 10 **subtract** 3 is 7
3 **less than** 10 is 7
(the **difference between** 10 and 3 is 7)

$4 \times 5 = 20$ 4 **multiplied by** 5 is 20
4 **times** 5 is 20
the **product of** 4 and 5 is 20
$20 \div 5 = 4$ 20 **divided by** 5 is 4

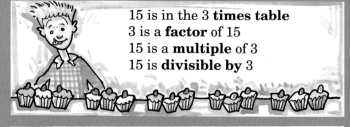

15 is in the 3 **times table**
3 is a **factor** of 15
15 is a **multiple** of 3
15 is **divisible by** 3

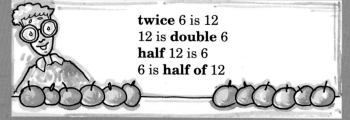

twice 6 is 12
12 is **double** 6
half 12 is 6
6 is **half of** 12

treble 6 is 18
a **third of** 18 is 6

I **estimate** that there are 29 eggs in the bowl.

84 is between 80 and 90, but is closer to 80.
We write 84 as 80 when we **round** to the nearest ten.

1 is the most important figure in 1683 as it is worth 1000. The 6 is the second most important figure as it is worth 600. But 1683 is nearer to 1700 than to 1600. When we **round** 1683 **to two significant figures**, or the two most important figures, we write 1700.

36.1278 is written as 36.128 when it is **rounded to three decimal places**.

A **rough answer** to 2.8×31 is given by rounding: $3 \times 30 = 90$.

3×30 is an **approximation** for 2.8×31.

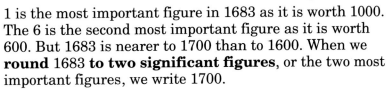

2.8×31 is $\begin{cases} \textbf{around} \\ \textbf{approximately} \\ \textbf{about} \end{cases}$ $3 \times 30 = 90$.

The $\begin{cases} \textbf{exact} \\ \textbf{correct} \\ \textbf{accurate} \end{cases}$ answer to 2.8×31 is 86.8.

We count and write numbers in groups of 10, that is, in **base** 10. For example 23 is 2 tens and 3 units. We can also count or write numbers in other bases. For example, 111 in base 2 means 1 four, 1 two and 1 unit, which is the same as seven.

5 is **equal to** $3 + 2$.   3 and 5 are unequal.

$2 \times 2 \times 2 \times 2 \times 2$ can be written as 2^5. This method of writing numbers is called the **index notation**.

The 5 is the **index** or **power**.

We read 2^5 as '2 to the power of 5'.

① building society

② bank

③ for hire

④ pay bit by bit

⑤ shop

HIGHLAND BEDS

HIRE-PURCHASE

SALE

SALE SALE £10 DEPOSIT

POST OFFICE

7 auction

8 reduced prices

SALE

DEPOSIT

9 money you pay at first

POST OFFICE **10** Post Office

6 market

11 cashpoint machine

Money

penny

two pence piece

five pence piece

ten pence piece

twenty pence piece

fifty pence piece

one pound coin

banknotes

12

I'm making a good **profit** today.

I'll be making a **loss**, I'm sure.

Do you think this is a **bargain**?

You won't get **value for money** there.

1 bargain

2 price/cost

3 4 The customer is **buying** and the stallholder is **selling**.

5 profit 6 loss

7 goods

1 postal order

2 collecting money

3 savings

4 child benefit

5 pension

6 stamps

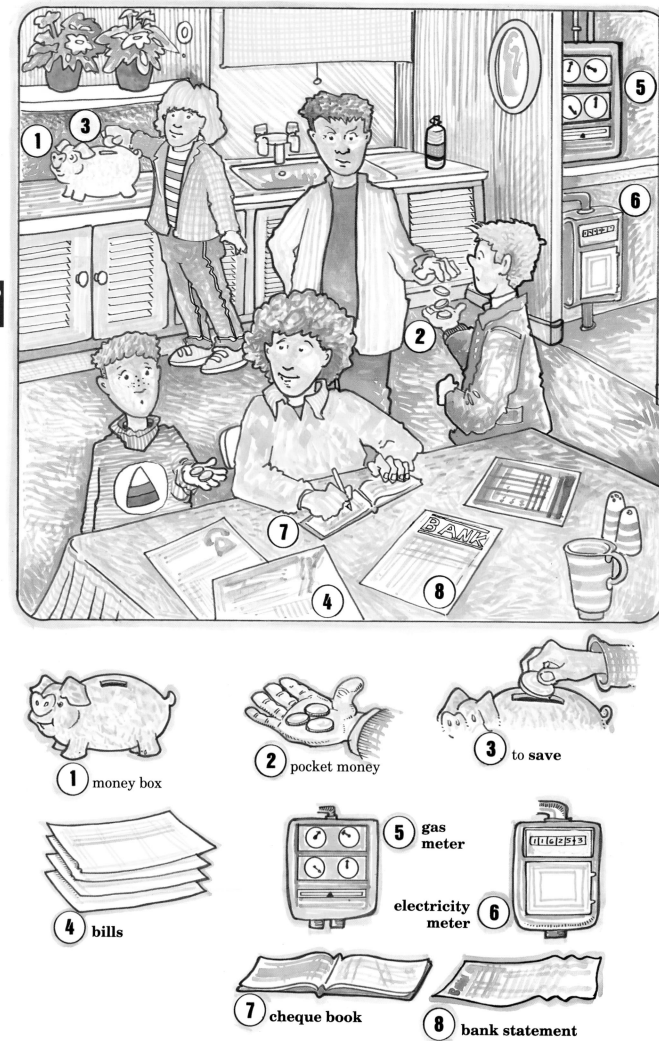

1. money box
2. pocket money
3. to **save**
4. bills
5. gas meter
6. electricity meter
7. cheque book
8. bank statement

Algebra

Factory output

(1) **straight-line graph**

(2) **vertical axis**

(3) **horizontal axis**

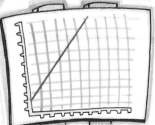

(4) **Pascal's triangle**

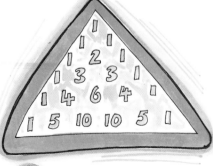

(5) **balance scales**

(6) The two sides of the scales **bal**

19

Number machine
Output = Input × 2

9

IN

OUT

8

7

10

11

12

13

---

8 input

9 Number machine
Output = Input × 2
formula/rule

10 output

7 number machine
function machine

12 horizontal

11 vertical

13 symbols

In an **equation**, both sides must balance: $5 + 3 = 2 + 6$.

In some equations, we don't know the value of one of the numbers: $? + 6 = 10$

We need to discover the value of ?; that is, we need to **solve** the equation. By doing this, we discover the **unknown number** (or the missing number).

Sometimes, we use a letter, such as x, to represent an unknown number. An equation, like the one above, is called a **linear equation**.

Some equations contain **brackets**. We must calculate the part inside the brackets first:
$(2 \times 3) - 5 + (4 - 2) = 6 - 5 + 2 = 3$

x^2 means $x \times x$. x^3 means $x \times x \times x$. The 2 (and the 3) is called the **index** or the **power**. An equation that includes x^2 or x^3 (or larger powers) is called a **polynomial equation**.

Pascal's triangle is a triangular arrangement of numbers where each number is the total of the two numbers above it.

This is the **Fibonacci sequence**:

The rule for this sequence is that the next number is the total of the two preceding numbers.

When we discover a pattern or find a rule, we are **generalising**.

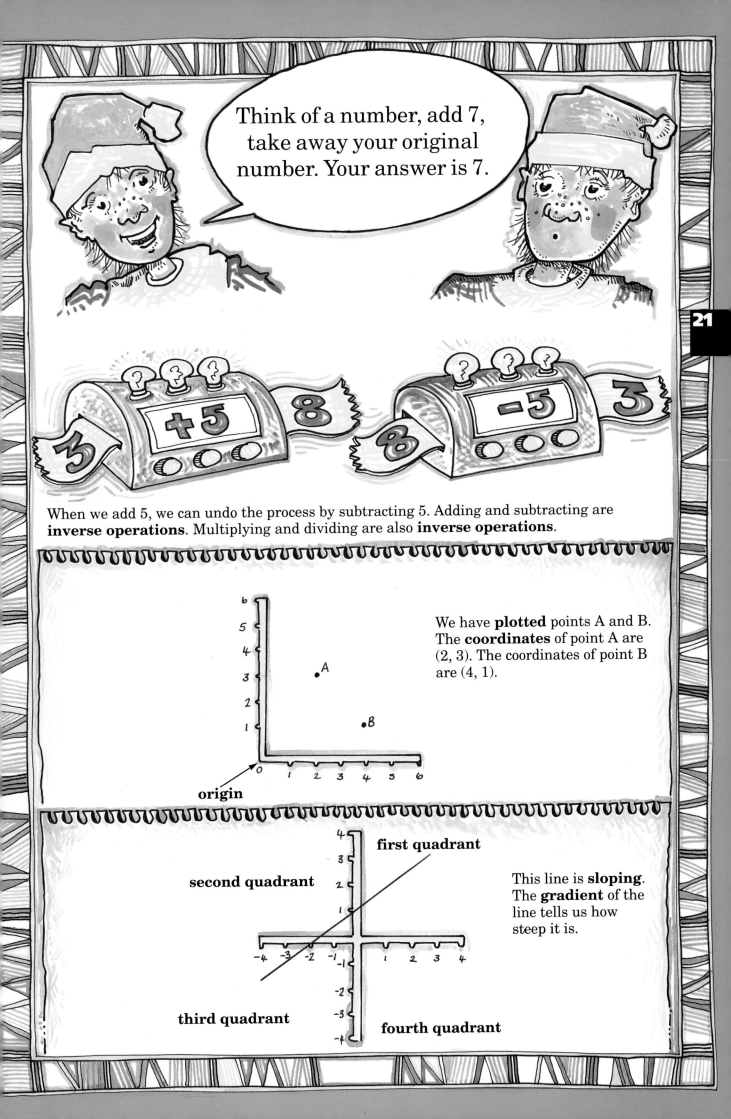

Think of a number, add 7, take away your original number. Your answer is 7.

When we add 5, we can undo the process by subtracting 5. Adding and subtracting are **inverse operations**. Multiplying and dividing are also **inverse operations**.

We have **plotted** points A and B. The **coordinates** of point A are (2, 3). The coordinates of point B are (4, 1).

origin

first quadrant

second quadrant

third quadrant

fourth quadrant

This line is **sloping**. The **gradient** of the line tells us how steep it is.

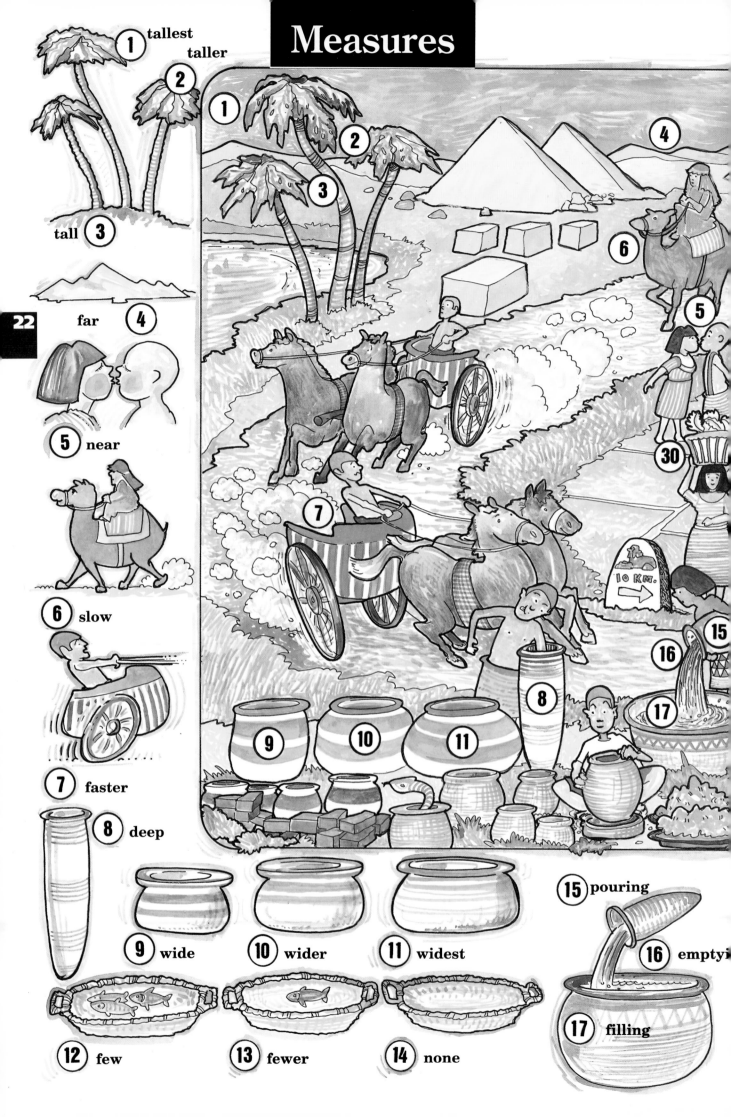

Measures

tallest
taller

1
2
3 tall

far 4

5 near

6 slow

7 faster

8 deep

9 wide
10 wider
11 widest

12 few
13 fewer
14 none

15 pouring
16 emptyi[ng]
17 filling

22

10 Km.

30

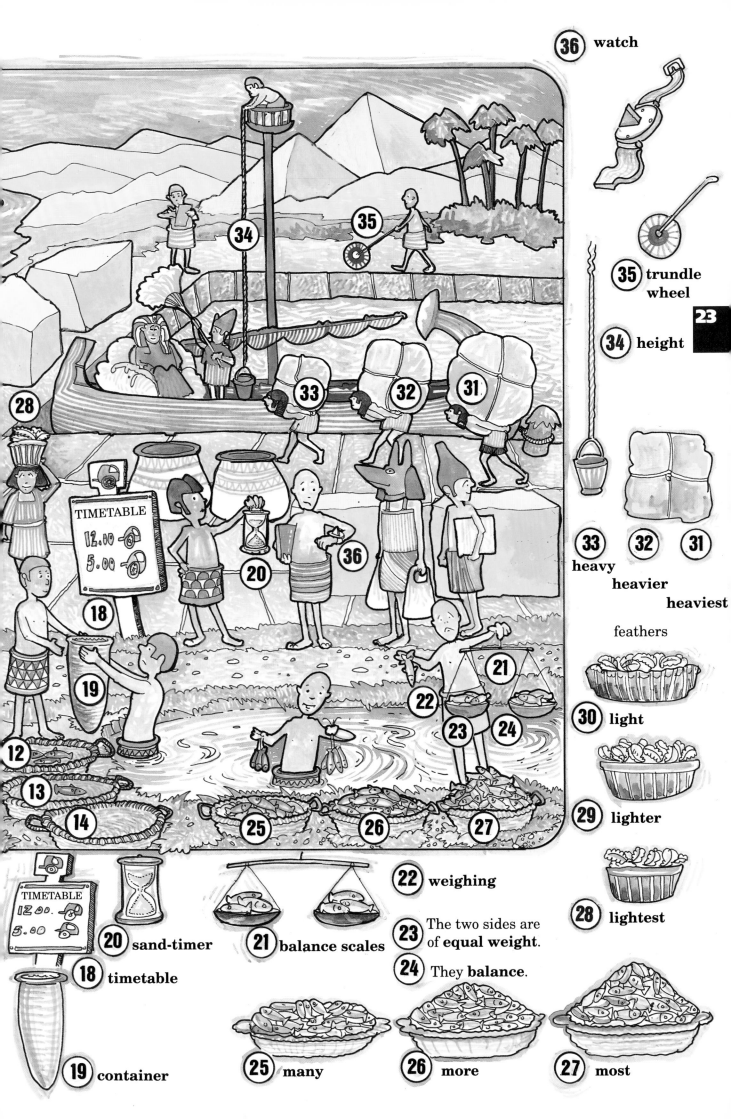

36 watch

35 trundle wheel

23

34 height

33 heavy

32 heavier

31 heaviest

feathers

30 light

29 lighter

28 lightest

TIMETABLE
12.00
5.00

22 weighing

21 balance scales

23 The two sides are of **equal weight**.

24 They **balance**.

20 sand-timer

18 timetable

TIMETABLE
12.00
5.00

19 container

25 many

26 more

27 most

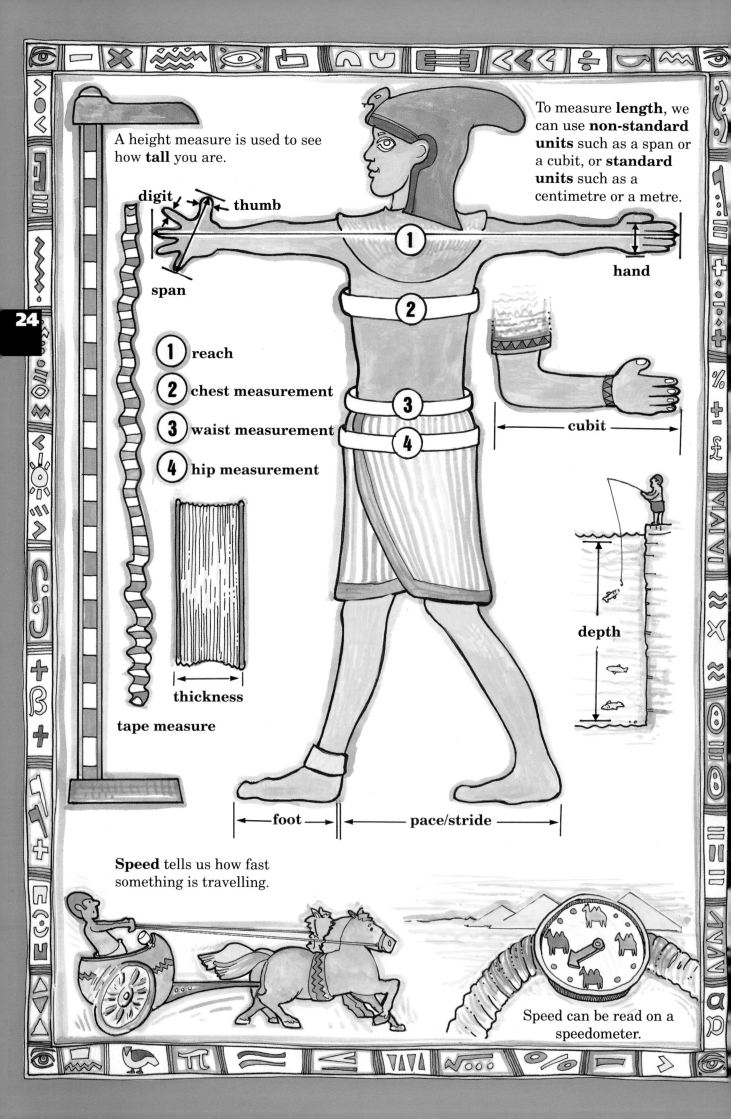

A height measure is used to see how **tall** you are.

To measure **length**, we can use **non-standard units** such as a span or a cubit, or **standard units** such as a centimetre or a metre.

digit

thumb

span

hand

① reach

② chest measurement

③ waist measurement

④ hip measurement

cubit

thickness

tape measure

depth

foot

pace/stride

Speed tells us how fast something is travelling.

Speed can be read on a speedometer.

24

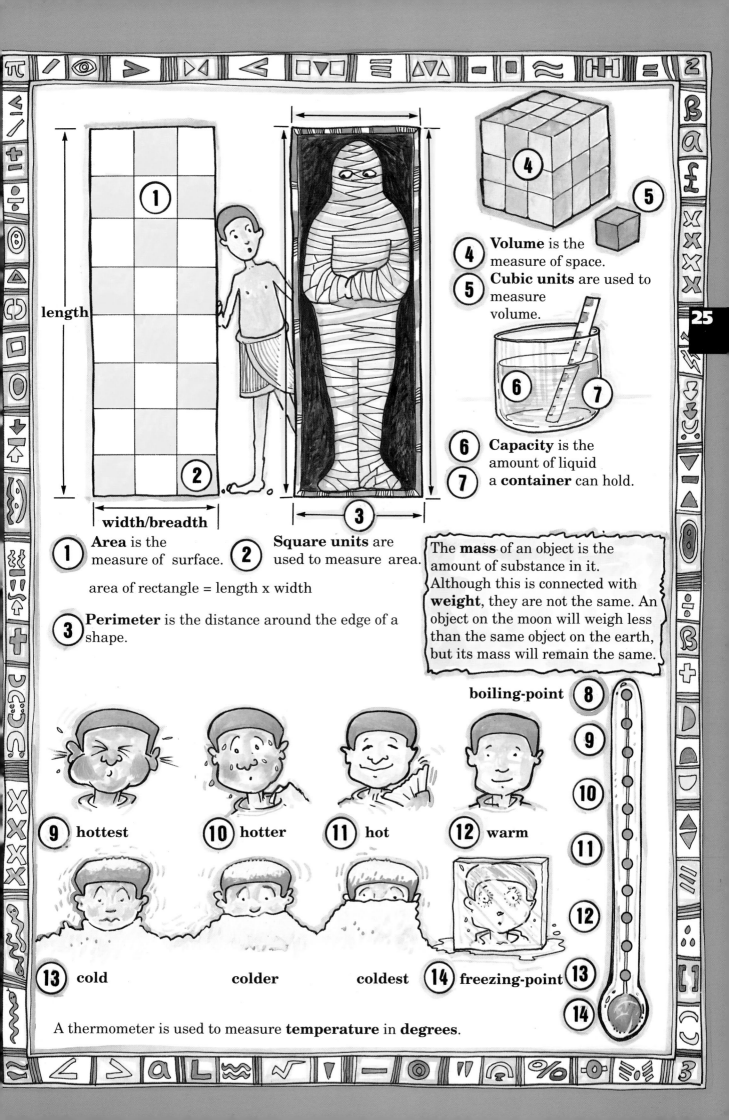

length

width/breadth

Volume is the measure of space.

Cubic units are used to measure volume.

Capacity is the amount of liquid a **container** can hold.

(1) **Area** is the measure of surface.

(2) **Square units** are used to measure area.

area of rectangle = length x width

(3) **Perimeter** is the distance around the edge of a shape.

The **mass** of an object is the amount of substance in it. Although this is connected with **weight**, they are not the same. An object on the moon will weigh less than the same object on the earth, but its mass will remain the same.

boiling-point (8)

(9) **hottest**   (10) **hotter**   (11) **hot**   (12) **warm**

(13) **cold**   **colder**   **coldest**   (14) **freezing-point**

A thermometer is used to measure **temperature** in **degrees**.

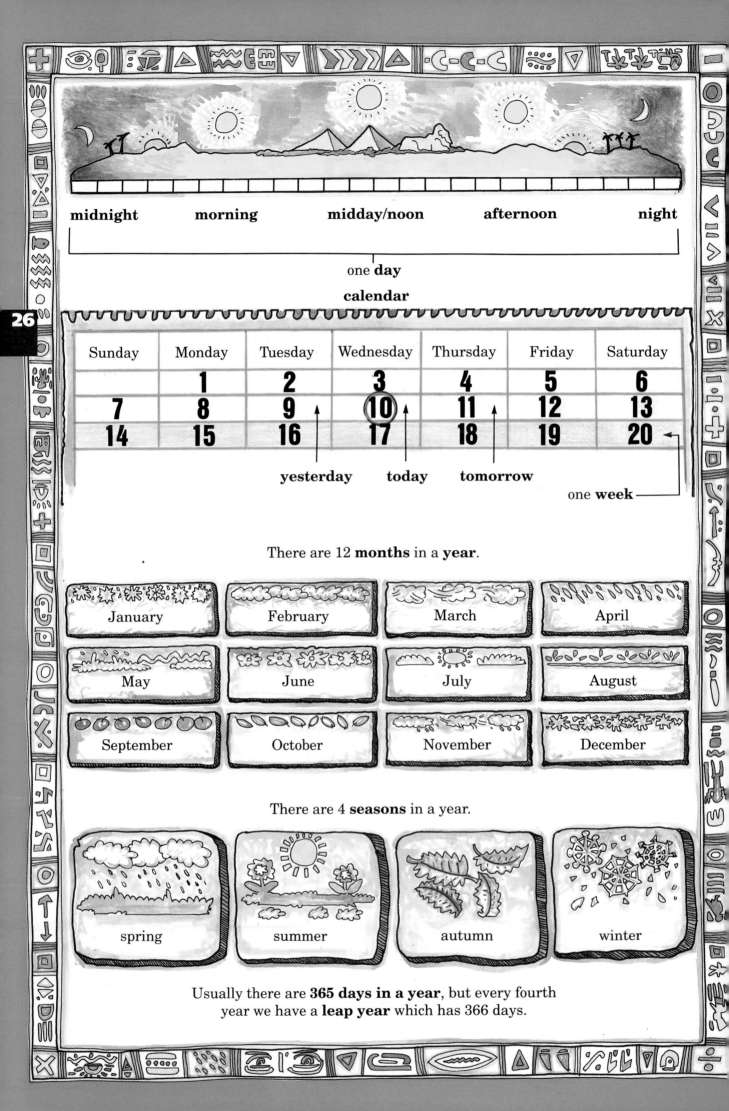

midnight   morning   midday/noon   afternoon   night

one **day**

calendar

Sunday	Monday	Tuesday	Wednesday	Thursday	Friday	Saturday
	1	2	3	4	5	6
7	8	9	⑩	11	12	13
14	15	16	17	18	19	20

yesterday   today   tomorrow

one **week**

There are 12 **months** in a **year**.

January	February	March	April
May	June	July	August
September	October	November	December

There are 4 **seasons** in a year.

| spring | summer | autumn | winter |

Usually there are **365 days in a year**, but every fourth
year we have a **leap year** which has 366 days.

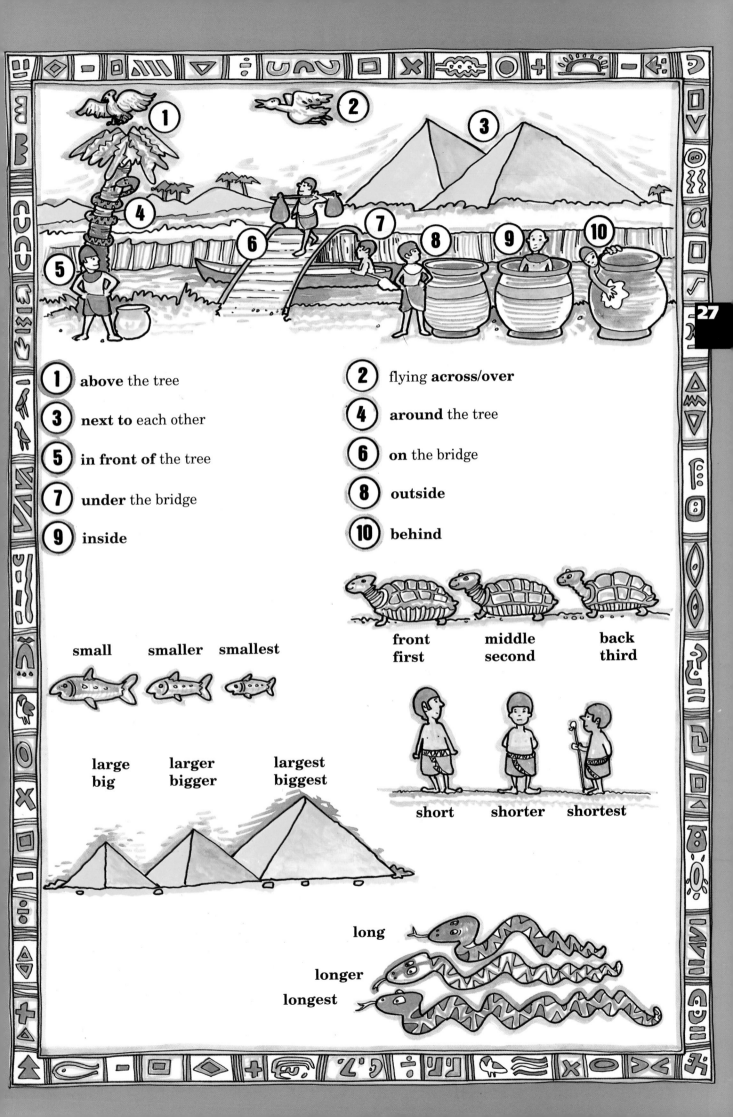

1 **above** the tree

2 flying **across/over**

3 **next to** each other

4 **around** the tree

5 **in front of** the tree

6 **on** the bridge

7 **under** the bridge

8 **outside**

9 inside

10 behind

small   smaller   smallest

large   larger   largest
big   bigger   biggest

front   middle   back
first   second   third

short   shorter   shortest

long

longer
longest

27

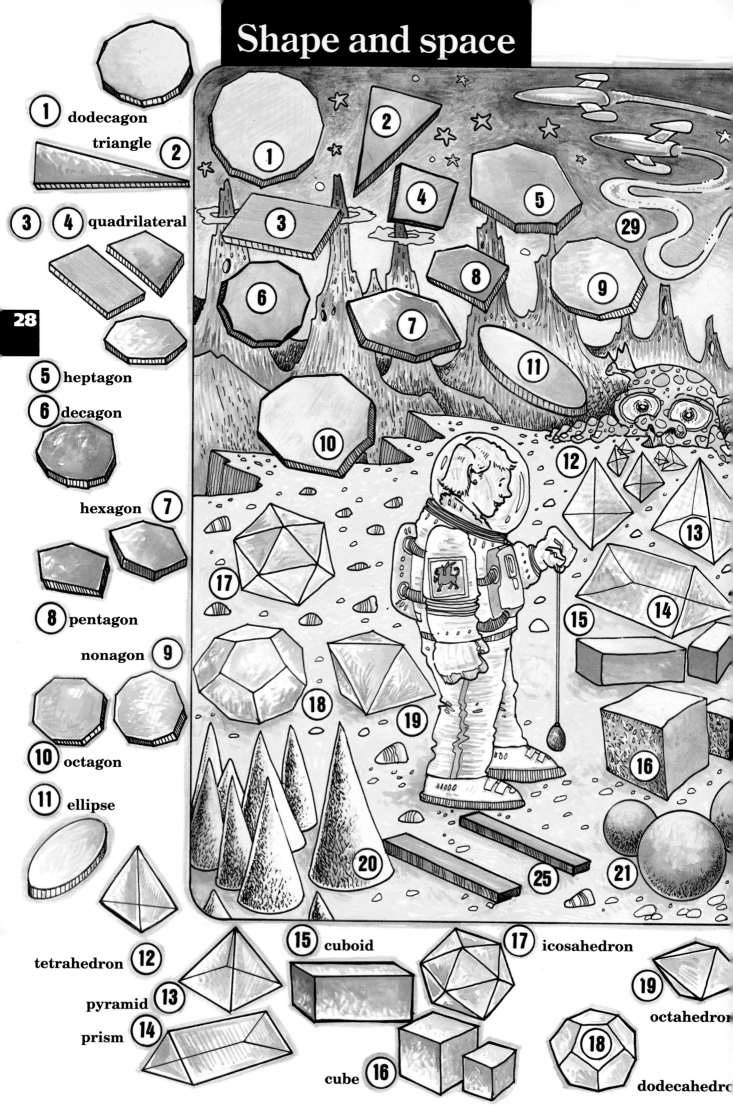

Shape and space

28

① dodecagon
② triangle
③ ④ quadrilateral
⑤ heptagon
⑥ decagon
hexagon ⑦
⑧ pentagon
nonagon ⑨
⑩ octagon
⑪ ellipse

tetrahedron ⑫
pyramid ⑬
prism ⑭
⑮ cuboid
cube ⑯
⑰ icosahedron
⑱ dodecahedron
⑲ octahedron

36 spiral

35 pentagram

hexagram

34

shape with **rotational symmetry**

33

shape with **reflective symmetry**

32

31 curved line

30 curve

29 twisting line

vertical **28**

27 horizontal

26

perpendicular

25 parallel

24 tessellation

20 cone

22 cylinder

23 tetrominoes

21 sphere

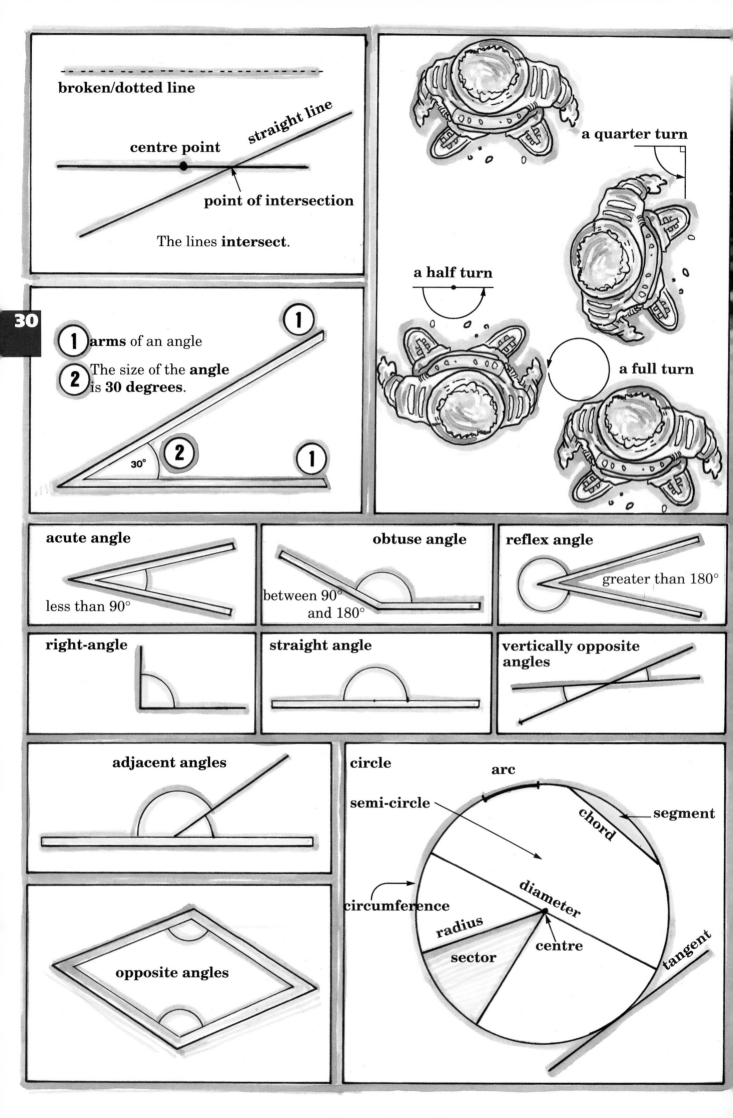

broken/dotted line

straight line

centre point

point of intersection

The lines **intersect**.

30

1 **arms** of an angle

2 The size of the **angle** is **30 degrees**.

30°

a quarter turn

a half turn

a full turn

acute angle

less than 90°

obtuse angle

between 90° and 180°

reflex angle

greater than 180°

right-angle

straight angle

vertically opposite angles

adjacent angles

opposite angles

circle

arc

semi-circle

chord

segment

circumference

diameter

radius

centre

sector

tangent

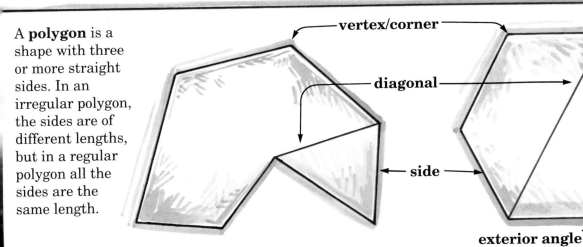

A **polygon** is a shape with three or more straight sides. In an irregular polygon, the sides are of different lengths, but in a regular polygon all the sides are the same length.

vertex/corner

diagonal

side

interior angle

exterior angle

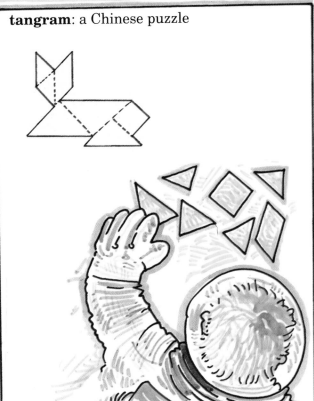

tangram: a Chinese puzzle

Scalene triangle: all three sides are different lengths.

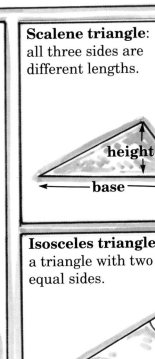

height

base

Equilateral triangle: all three sides are equal.

60°

60° 60°

Isosceles triangle: a triangle with two equal sides.

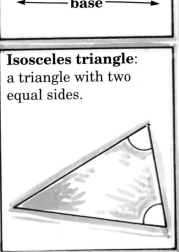

Right-angled triangle: one of the three angles is a right-angle.

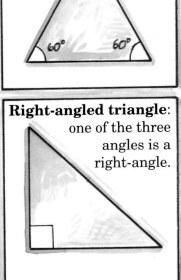

Kite: two pairs of adjacent sides equal.

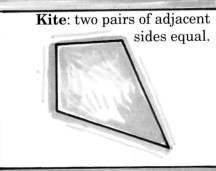

Parallelogram: two pairs of opposite sides parallel and equal.

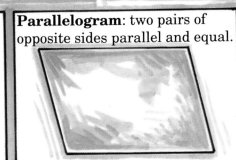

Rectangle: four sides and four right-angles,

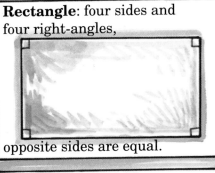

opposite sides are equal.

Rhombus: four equal sides, opposite sides parallel.

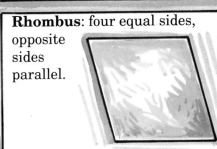

Square: four equal sides and four right-angles.

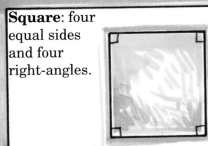

Trapezium: four sides, one pair of opposite sides parallel.

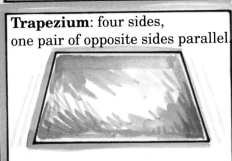

Symmetrical shapes

This shape has **reflective symmetry**.

mirror line   line of symmetry

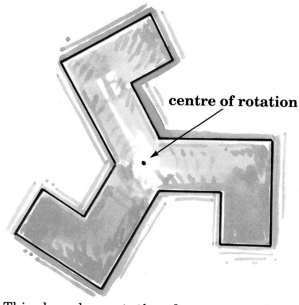

centre of rotation

This shape has **rotational symmetry**. In one rotation, it fits into its outline three times. The **order of symmetry** of this shape is 3.

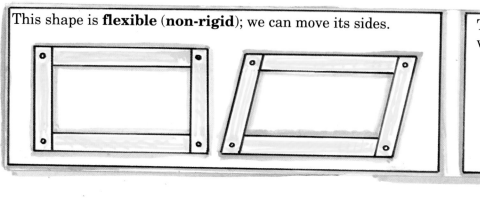

This shape is **flexible** (**non-rigid**); we can move its sides.

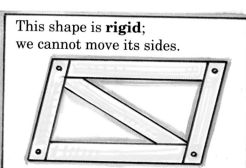

This shape is **rigid**; we cannot move its sides.

open figure

closed figure

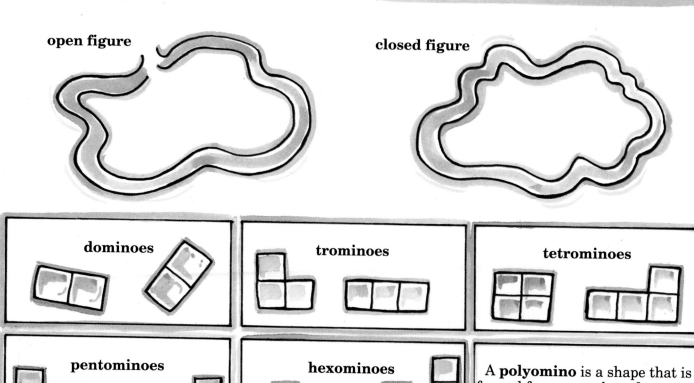

dominoes	trominoes	tetrominoes

pentominoes	hexominoes	A **polyomino** is a shape that is formed from a number of squares.

A **solid** is a three-dimensional shape.

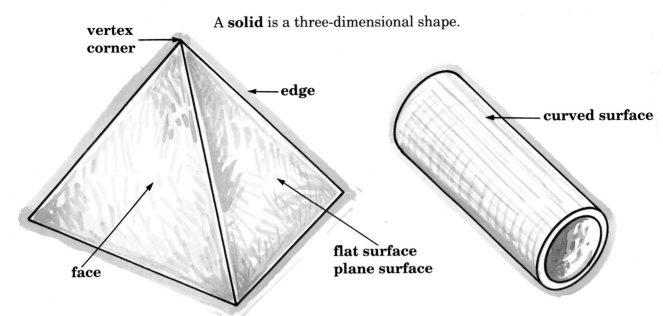

vertex
corner

edge

curved surface

face

flat surface
plane surface

A **polyhedron** is a solid whose faces are all polygons.

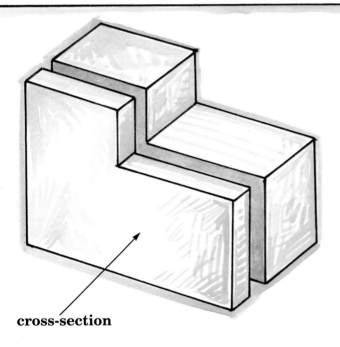

cross-section

A **net** is a two-dimensional shape which may be
folded to form a three-dimensional shape.

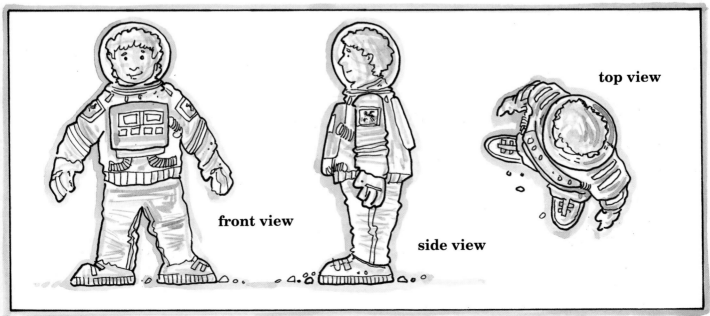

top view

front view

side view

Transformations

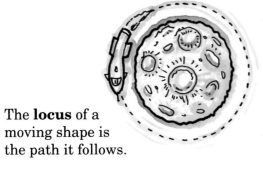

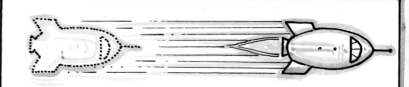

The **locus** of a moving shape is the path it follows.

In a **translation**, the shape moves in a straight line.

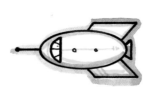 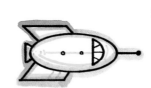

In a **reflection**, the shape is reflected in the line of reflection.

In a **rotation**, the shape is rotated about the centre of rotation.

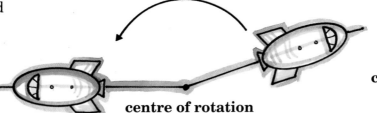

centre of rotation

clockwise

anticlockwise

In an **enlargement,** the shape is made bigger or smaller according to the **scale factor**.

scale factor: $\times 2$

scale factor: $\times \frac{1}{2}$

up

down

to the **left**   to the **right**

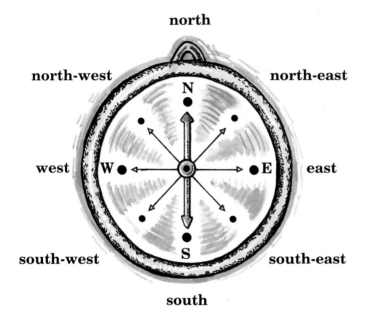

north

north-west   **north-east**

N

west W   E **east**

S

south-west   **south-east**

south

A compass shows the **direction** of the north.

The **points of the compass** are used to show direction. Sometimes they are written in the form of a bearing.

The **bearing** 030° means 30° to the east of north.

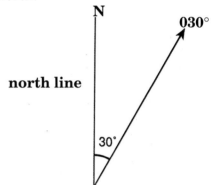

N   **030°**

north line

30°

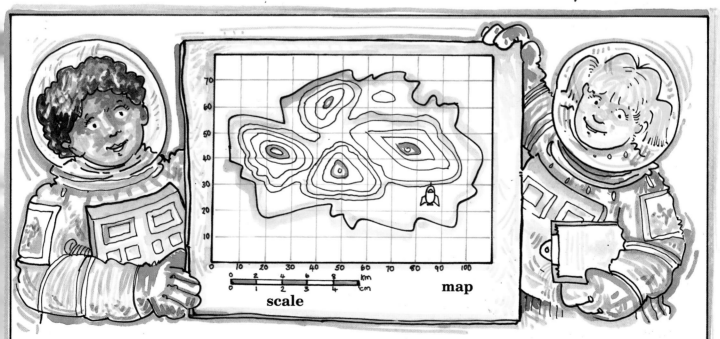

scale   **map**

The **grid reference** of the rocket is 8525.

Do you live in this town?

Yes ☐

No ☐

Sean is conducting a survey by collecting **data** (or facts).
He asks a number of people to complete a questionnaire.

Sean uses the responses to form a **frequency table**:

	Tally	Number
Residents	I I I	3
Day trippers	⑅HT I	6
Holidaymakers	I I I I	4

↑ Tally mark

The study of the data collected is called **statistics**.

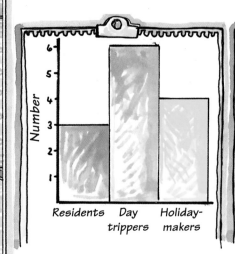

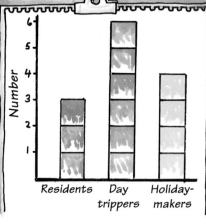

The information may also be shown as a **bar graph**

or a **block graph**

or a **bar-line graph**

Age in years	Tally	Number	Angle
0 – 12	HHT III	8	96°
13 – 17	IIII	4	48°
18 – 25	III	3	36°
26 – 39	HHT II	7	84°
40 – 60	II	2	24°
60+	HHT I	6	72°

Kerry has been conducting a survey of the ages of different people. The ages vary from 7 years to 72 years. The range of the ages is 65 (72 – 7).

The **range** is the difference between the largest and smallest numbers in a set.

In this frequency table, the data has been **grouped** because the age range is so great. Data is usually put into equal **groups** (or **classes**). The size of the group is called the **class interval**. Here the groups are different sizes.

Kerry presents the results as a **pie chart**.

A group of children have been collecting and **sorting** sea shells.

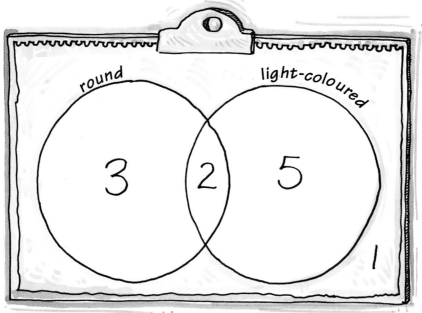

round light-coloured

3   2   5

1

Venn diagram

Seven shells are **members of the set** of light-coloured shells.
Five shells are members of the set of round shells.
The two sets **intersect**. There are two light-coloured round shells.

	round	long
light-coloured	2	5
dark-coloured	3	1

Here are other ways of displaying the information.

Carroll diagram

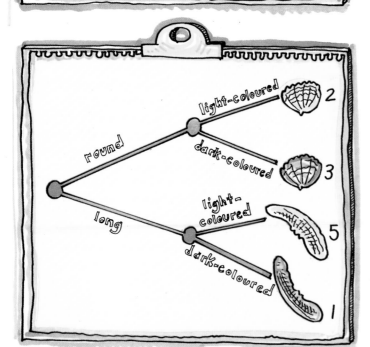

round — light-coloured — 2
— dark-coloured — 3
long — light-coloured — 5
— dark-coloured — 1

Tree diagram

Pictogram

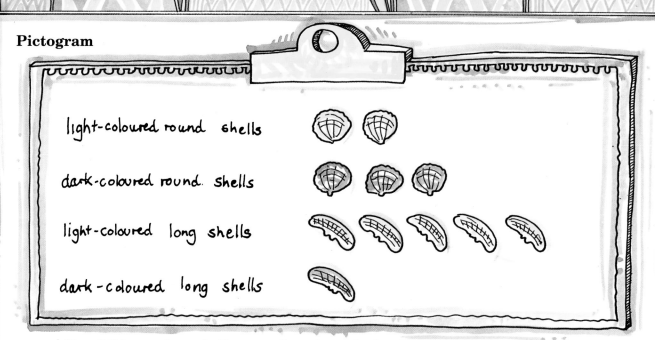

light-coloured round shells

dark-coloured round shells

light-coloured long shells

dark-coloured long shells

The children take a shell **at random** from the bag. They make a **random choice**.

What is the **probability** of choosing a marble?

None – that's **impossible**.

We are **certain** of taking a shell from the bag. It is **probable** (or **likely**) that it will be a light-coloured shell.

marble	dark shell		light shell	shell
	unlikely/improbable	even chance evens	likely/probable	
0		½		1
impossible	poor chance		good chance	certain

Probability Scale

	Ice cream	Flake	Sauce
Mary	✓		✓
David	✓	✓	✓
Gaynor	✓	✓	

This table shows some possible combinations when choosing ice cream. Such a table is called a **two-way table**.

We often wish to obtain some general information about the data collected. One way of doing this is to calculate the **average**. There are three methods of finding the average value:

Number of fish caught:
1, 2, 3, 3, 5, 6, 8

Median = 3
Mean = 28 ÷ 7 = 4
Mode = 3

The **median** is the value that lies in the middle after the numbers have been put in order.
The **mean** is the total of the numbers divided by how many numbers there are.
The **mode** is the most frequent value.

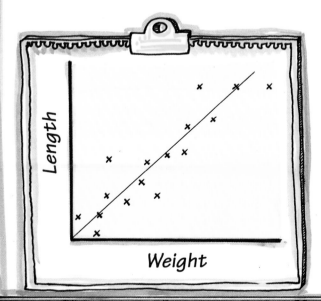

The number of fish is an example of **discrete data**. The number can be 0, 1, 2, 3, ... but cannot be 2.5 or 3.1.
The length of a fish is an example of **continuous data**. The length can be 23.6 cm or 48.16 cm, or any other reasonable value.

A **scatter graph** is a way of representing information when both values vary.

An **unbiased** dice is a fair dice. Each number is equally likely to be thrown.

This is a **biased** dice. We are more likely to throw a 2 than a 3.

A **random number** is a number chosen at random.

Bingo is an example of a **game of chance**. Winning depends on the random choice of numbers, not on the skill of players.

Two **events** are **independent** of each other if the result of one has no effect on the result of the other. Throwing a dice and tossing a coin are independent events.

A **network** is a diagram of connecting lines.

There are 6 **nodes**, 9 **arcs** and 5 **regions** in this network. This network may be traversed (drawn without lifting the pencil).

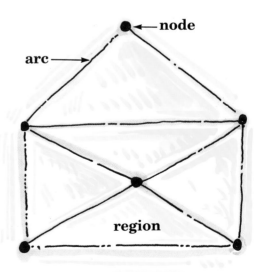

node

arc

region

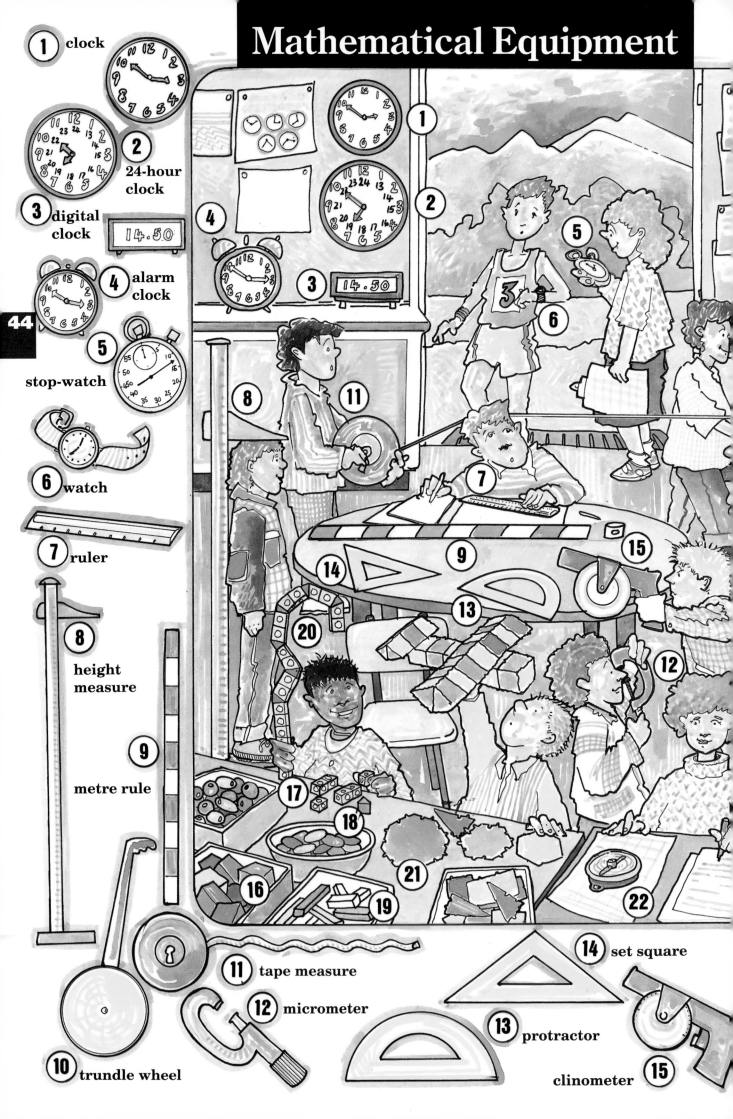

Mathematical Equipment

1. clock
2. 24-hour clock
3. digital clock
4. alarm clock
5. stop-watch
6. watch
7. ruler
8. height measure
9. metre rule
10. trundle wheel
11. tape measure
12. micrometer
13. protractor
14. set square
15. clinometer

44

29 decimal abacus

28 abacus

27 dice

26 spinner

25 measuring jug

24 measuring cylinder

23 compasses

22 compass

21 shape equipment

20 interlocking shapes

19 rods

18 counters

17 beads

16 blocks

45

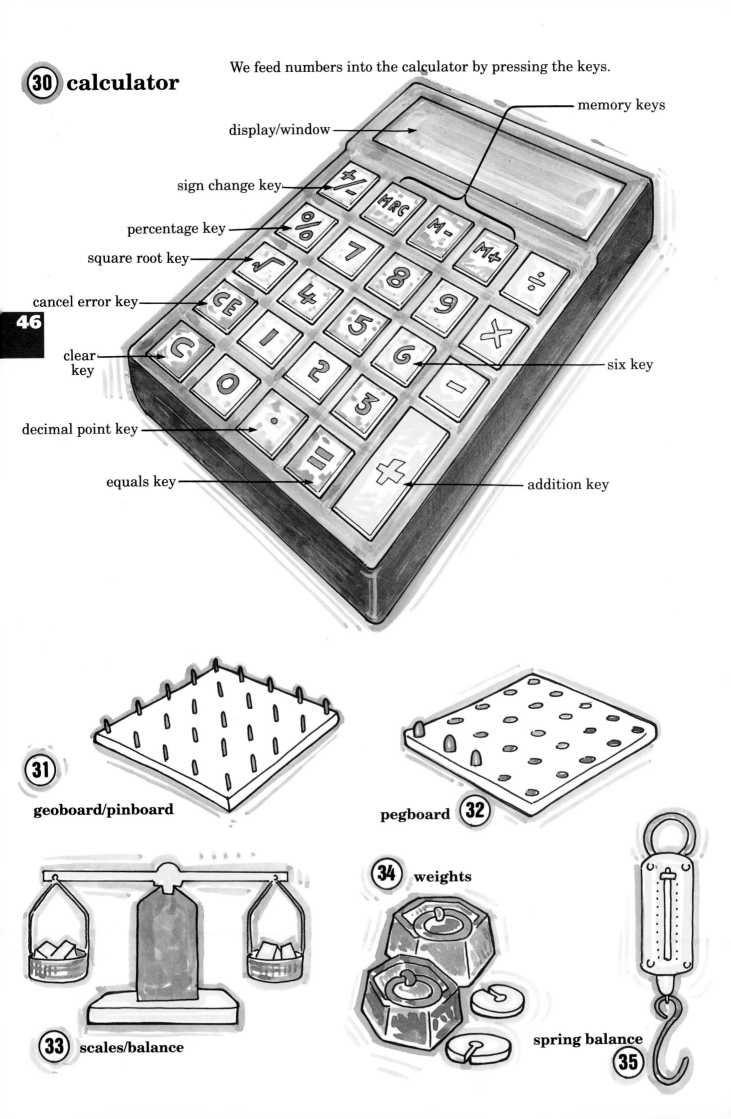

30 calculator

We feed numbers into the calculator by pressing the keys.

memory keys

display/window

sign change key

percentage key

square root key

cancel error key

46

clear key

decimal point key

equals key

six key

addition key

31

geoboard/pinboard

pegboard 32

34 weights

33 scales/balance

spring balance

35

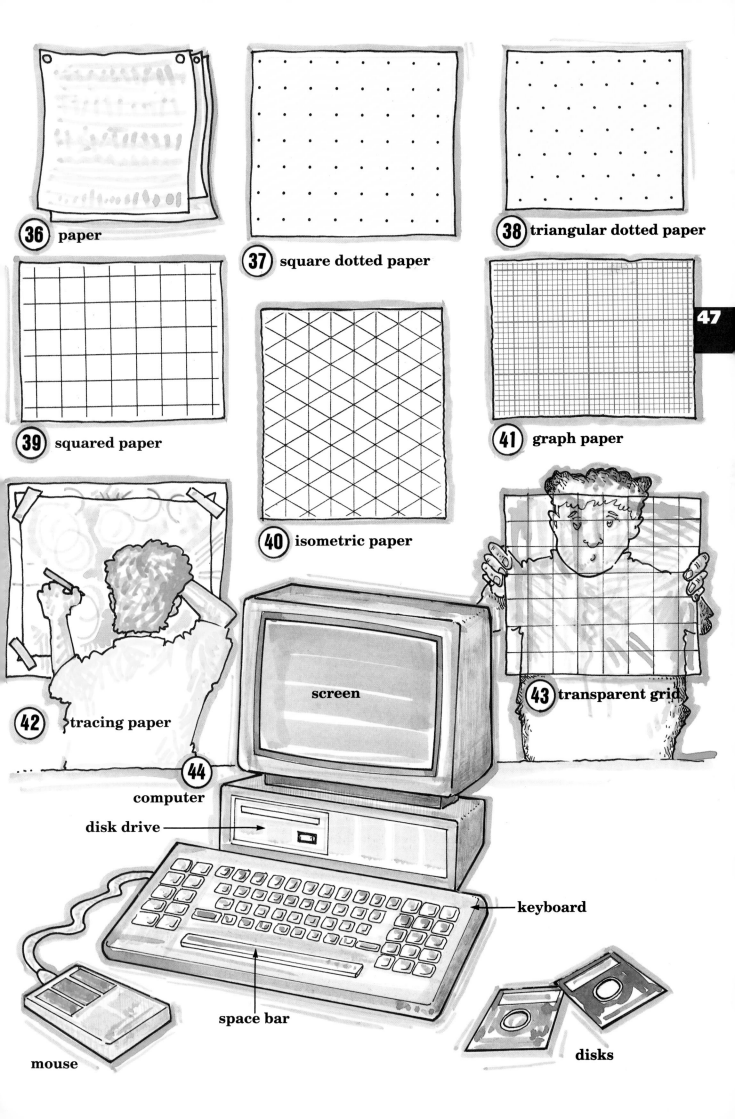

36 paper

37 square dotted paper

38 triangular dotted paper

39 squared paper

40 isometric paper

41 graph paper

42 tracing paper

43 transparent grid

44 computer

screen

disk drive

keyboard

space bar

mouse

disks

Useful Information

Symbols

48

=	equal to (equals sign)	√	square root
≠	not equal to	³√	cube root
≐ ≈	approximately equal to	π	'pi' (3.14...)
≡	exactly equal to	10°	10 degrees
>	greater than	26'	26 minutes
<	less than	42''	42 seconds
≥	greater than or equal to	%	per cent
≤	less than or equal to	.	decimal point
+	add/plus	∟	right-angle
–	subtract/minus	∠	angle
×	multiply	△	triangle
÷	divide	△	equal lines
/	divide	⇉	parallel lines
±	add or subtract (plus or minus)	||	parallel to
£	pound	⊥	perpendicular to
5^2	5 squared	∴	therefore
5^3	5 cubed		

Abbreviations

a.m.	ante meridiem, in the morning
°C	degrees Celsius, degrees centigrade
cm	centimetre
cm^2	square centimetre
cm^3	cubic centimetre
dm	decimetre
E	east
°F	degrees Fahrenheit
g	gram/gramme
kg	kilogram
km	kilometre
l	litre
L.C.M.	lowest common multiple
m	metre
mg	milligram
ml	millilitre
mm	millimetre
m.p.h.	miles per hour
N	north
NE	north-east
NW	north-west
p	pence
p.m.	post meridiem, in the afternoon or evening
S	south
SE	south-east
SW	south-west
V.A.T.	Value Added Tax
W	west
2-D	two-dimensional
3-D	three-dimensional

Metric and Imperial Units

Imperial units

Length

12 inches   = 1 foot
3 feet   = 1 yard
1760 yards = 1 mile

Area

144 square inches   = 1 square foot
9 square feet   = 1 square yard
4840 square yards   = 1 acre
640 acres   = 1 square mile

Weight

16 ounces   = 1 pound
14 pounds   = 1 stone
112 pounds   = 8 stones
              = 1 hundredweight
2240 pounds = 20 hundredweight
              = 1 ton

Capacity

4 gills = 1 pint
2 pints = 1 quart
8 pints = 4 quarts
          = 1 gallon

Metric Units

Length

10 millimetres	= 1 centimetre
10 centimetres	= 1 decimetre
100 centimetres	= 10 decimetres
	= 1 metre
10 metres	= 1 decametre
10 decametres	= 1 hectometre
1000 metres	= 10 hectometres
	= 1 kilometre

Weight

10 milligrams	= 1 centigram
10 centigrams	= 1 decigram
1000 milligrams	= 10 decigrams
	= 1 gram
10 grams	= 1 decagram
10 decagrams	= 1 hectogram
1000 grams	= 10 hectograms
	= 1 kilogram
1000 kilograms	= 1 tonne (metric ton)

Area

100 square millimetres	= 1 square centimetre
10 000 square centimetres	= 1 square metre
10 000 square metres	= 1 hectare
100 hectares	= 1 square kilometre

Capacity

10 millilitres	= 1 centilitre
10 centilitres	= 1 decilitre
1000 millilitres	= 10 decilitres
	= 1 litre
10 litres	= 1 decalitre
10 decalitres	= 1 hectolitre
1000 litres	= 10 hectolitres
	= 1 kilolitre

Volume

1000 cubic centimetres	= 1 cubic decimetre
1 000 000 cubic centimetres	= 1000 cubic decimetres
	= 1 cubic metre

Conversion tables

Metric → Imperial

1 centimetre	= 0.394 inches
1 metre	= 1.094 yards
1 kilometre	= 0.6214 miles
1 hectare	= 2.471 acres
1 square kilometre	= 0.386 square mile
1 litre	= 1.76 pints
1 litre	= 0.22 gallons
1 gram	= 0.035 ounces
1 kilogram	= 2.205 pounds
1 tonne	= 0.984 ton

Imperial → Metric

1 inch	= 2.54 centimetres
1 foot	= 30.48 centimetres
1 yard	= 0.9144 metres
1 mile	= 1.609 kilometres
1 acre	= 0.405 hectares
1 square mile	= 2.59 square kilometres
1 pint	= 0.568 litres
1 gallon	= 4.546 litres
1 ounce	= 28.35 grams
1 pound	= 453.59 grams
1 hundredweight	= 50.8 kilograms
1 ton	= 1.016 tonnes

Other Units

Angle Measures

60 seconds (60") = 1 minute (1')
60 minutes (60') = 1 degree (1°)
360 degrees (360°) = 1 complete rotation

Temperature

Boiling point for water: 212°F or 100°C
Freezing point for water: 32°F or 0°C

Time

60 seconds = 1 minute
60 minutes = 1 hour
24 hours = 1 day
7 days = 1 week
12 months = 1 year
52 weeks = 1 year
365 days = 1 year (366 in a leap year)
10 years = 1 decade
100 years = 1 century

Thirty days have September,
April, June and November;
All the rest have thirty-one
Excepting February alone,
Which has but twenty-eight days clear,
And twenty-nine in each leap year.

Index

The following is an alphabetical list of words that you may come across when you are doing Mathematics. The page numbers show where these words are illustrated in the book.

The list also shows you whether the words are nouns, adjectives, verbs, adverbs or prepositions.

KEY
adj - adjective
n - noun
npl - plural noun
v - verb
adv - adverb
prep - preposition

55

season, n, 26
second, n, 4 (position); 48, 53 (time)
sector, n, 30
segment, n, 30
semi-circle, n, 30
septagon, n, 28
sequence, n, 8
    Fibonacci sequence, 20
set, n, 3, 40
    subset, 3
set square, 44
shape, n, 28-35
side, n, 31
    side view, 33
sieve of Eratosthenes, 6
sign (plus, minus), n, 5
sign change key, 46
significant figure, 9
sloping, adv, 21
solve, v, 20
south, n, 35, 49
    south-east, 35, 49
    south-west, 35, 49
span, n, 24
speed, n, 24
sphere, n, 29
spiral, n, 29
spring balance, 46
square, n, 31
square measures, 50, 51, 52
square number, 5
square root, 5, 48
square unit, 25
squared, adj, 48
standard unit, 24
statistics, npl, 38
stone, n, 50
straight angle, 30
straight line, 30
straight-line graph, 18
stride, n, 24
subset, n, 3
subtract, v, 8, 48
sum, n, 8
surface, n, 33
survey, n, 38
symbol, n, 19, 48
symmetrical, adj, 32
symmetry, n, 29, 32

T

table, n, 8
    frequency table, 38
    two-way table, 42
take away, v, 8
tally marks, 38
tangent, n, 30
tangram, n, 31

temperature, n, 25, 53
tessellation, n, 29
tetrahedron, n, 28
tetromino, n, 29, 32
thermometer, n, 25
thousand, n, 4
three-dimensional, adj, 33, 49
times, 8
timetable, n, 23
ton, n, 50, 52
tonne, n, 51, 52
top-heavy fraction, 7
top view, 33
transformation, n, 34
translation, n, 34
trapezium, n, 31
traverse, v, 43
tree diagram, 40
triangle, n, 28, 31, 48
    Pascal's triangle, 18, 20
triangular number, 5
tromino, n, 32
turn, n, 30
two-dimensional, adj, 33, 49
two-way table, 42

U

unbiased, adj, 43
unequal, adj, 9
units, npl, 24, 25, 50-52
unlikely, adj, 41

V

Venn diagram, 40
vertex, n, 31, 33
vertical, adj, 19, 29
vertically opposite angles, 30
volume, n, 25, 50, 51

W

west, n, 35, 49
whole number, 5
width, n, 25

Y

yard, n, 50, 52
    square yard, 50
year, n, 26, 53
    leap year, 26, 53

Z

zero, n, 4

58